The MAGNIFICENT 7

Great Composers in Song

MUSIC ARRANGED BY
John Carter

LYRICS, NARRATION AND ACTIVITY SHEETS BY
Mary Kay Beall

RECORDING ORCHESTRATED AND PRODUCED BY
Alan Billingsley

MUSICAL SEQUENCE

Alfred

Cover photos: Archive für Kunst und Geschichte, London
Book design/illustrations: Tanya Maiboroda

MEET JOHN CARTER and MARY KAY BEALL

John Carter and Mary Kay Beall are not only husband and wife, but they collaborate on a full-time basis on musical works of all kinds. They have been writing as a team since 1978 and have created several hundred pieces of music together. John Carter is recognized as one of the most productive and skillful writers in choral composition today. Before he and Mary Kay began their collaboration, he had nearly 200 published works to his credit.

John and Mary Kay write music for choirs of all types and of all ages . . . Elementary, Junior High, High School, College and Church. Many of their works are commissioned by various groups across the country to be performed for commemorative occasions. As a team, the Carters have produced a dozen musicals and a sacred opera in addition to their many choral works. They have been widely performed and their music exhibits a broad versatility of writing styles.

Mary Kay and John are members of ASCAP and the American Choral Directors Association. They have received ASCAP awards annually since 1984 for their ongoing contributions to choral literature. Together, they have over 30 years of public school teaching experience.

The Carters have been involved in church music for over 30 years as soloists, Directors of Music and sacred choral editors. Presently, they are Ministers of Music and Arts at the Northwest United Methodist Church in Columbus, Ohio. Mary Kay is also a student at Trinity Lutheran Seminary, pursuing a Master's Degree in Theological Studies.

1. OPENING FANFARE

Johann Sebastian Bach (1685-1750)

If you wanted to trace the Bach family back through five generations, you would find that nearly everyone in the family was a musician. JOHANN SEBASTIAN BACH was born on March 21, 1685, in Eisenach, Germany. He was the youngest of three sons born to Johann and Elizabeth. His mother died when he was only nine and a year later, as he was beginning to study the violin, his father passed away. So by the age of ten JOHANN SEBASTIAN was an orphan.

He was sent to live with his older brother, Johann Cristoph. Since money was tight, JOHANN SEBASTIAN was placed into a choir school where his tuition, room and board were paid and he could receive free musical training. He learned a lot about music there. When his voice changed and he could no longer sing in the Boys' Choir, he became the organist at the school.

From the very beginning BACH loved music. It is said that he once walked over two hundred miles to hear the famous organist Dietrich Buxtehude play a concert.

He worked in several churches throughout his life, writing music for his choirs and for the organ, sometimes a new piece every week. Many of the churches who hired him did not appreciate his talent. One church official said, "We can't use genius. What we need is someone to play the church music in a respectable and conventional manner."

In general, BACH was a happy person and great teacher. He was married twice and was a loving and playful father to his twenty children; many of them also became professional musicians.

BACH is one of the most important and productive musicians and composers who ever lived. In addition to hundreds of musical works, he is remembered for developing the Tempered Scale which we use when we tune keyboards today. Some of his most famous compositions include *Preludes and Fugues of the Well-Tempered Clavichord*, *Air for the G String*, *Toccata and Fugue in C minor*, *Mass in B minor*, and *The Brandenburg Concertos*.

Blind and in failing health, BACH died on July 28, 1750, of a stroke. The town newspaper carried only a brief notice of his death. His huge family was left without any inheritance and had to be supported by public charity. Sadly, his music lay unwanted in church cupboards where some of it was used to wrap sandwiches for students' picnic lunches. It was many years before the world realized what it had lost.

NARRATION

READER 1:   Long ago and far away
                        A boy named Bach was born one day.

READER 2:   He was a happy little kid
                        And music made him flip his lid.

READER 3:   He played the organ every Sunday;
                        Church was where he had his Fun Day.

READER 4:   His talents were, at least, unique.
                        He could write a tune a week!

ALL: Twenty children called him "Pappy."
                        His music makes the whole world happy.

2. WHEN YOU THINK OF BAROQUE MUSIC
("Jesu, Joy of Man's Desiring")

From Cantata 147
JOHANN SEBASTIAN BACH

Moderately (♩ = ca. 69-72)

1. When you think of Bar - oque mu - sic,
   tal - ent! What a gen - ius

J. S. Bach is some-one you should know.
at the or - gan or con-tin - u - o.

2. What a

Fugues, can - ta - tas, airs, _____ toc - ca - tas; Ev - 'ry

day a new _____ cre - a - tion. Twen - ty chil - dren,

all well - tem - pered, were his joy and

in - spir - a - tion.

Franz Joseph Haydn (1732-1809)

FRANZ JOSEPH HAYDN was born in Rohrau, Austria, on March 31, 1732, to a poor but deeply religious family. Neither of his parents were musicians and, with twelve children in the family, finances were always stretched. When HAYDN was five, his musical abilities began to be noticed. A cousin, Johann Matthias Frankh, who was a professional musician, offered to take charge of HAYDN'S musical training. Soon HAYDN became a member of the Boys' Choir at St. Stephen's Cathedral in Vienna. But when his voice changed at the age of fifteen, he was out of a job.

HAYDN took odd jobs to support himself, studied violin, harpsichord and voice, taught private students and studied the works of earlier composers. He was determined to be an important musician.

It wasn't long before HAYDN was hired as a valet and accompanist for an Italian opera composer, Nicolo Porpora, in exchange for music lessons. During his six years with Porpora, he wrote his first mass, his first opera and a string quartet.

HAYDN married Anna Maria Keller in 1760, although he had actually been in love with Anna's younger sister (who suddenly decided to enter a convent). Their marriage was not a happy one as Anna did not appreciate or understand her husband, insisting on using his manuscripts as curling paper. They separated after a few years, though HAYDN continued to provide for her.

HAYDN came in contact with many noble and wealthy people in town. In 1761 he was hired by Prince Esterhazy of Eisenstadt, Hungary, to conduct the choir and later the orchestra in the palace. This was a very desirable position which HAYDN enjoyed until 1790, composing some of his finest works and working sixteen hours each day.

HAYDN had many students including both Beethoven and Mozart, although Beethoven was such a difficult student that he didn't learn much from HAYDN. However, Mozart became a great friend and HAYDN even admitted that his own writing was influenced by Mozart's exceptional talents.

Respectfully called "Papa Haydn," the Father of the modern symphony orchestra, it was HAYDN who first divided the orchestra into four sections (strings, winds, brass and percussion), divisions we still use today. HAYDN also expanded the symphonic form from three to four movements by adding the minuet. He wrote over one thousand works in his lifetime, including *Farewell Symphony, Surprise Symphony, The Seasons* and *The Creation.*

After two musical appearances in London, HAYDN realized he could no longer travel due to failing health and advanced age. He spent his last years in Vienna where he was honored and revered. HAYDN had a happy temperament and strong religious beliefs. His music is full of fun and beautiful melodies.

NARRATION

READER 1: Papa Haydn was his name;
Music was his claim to fame.

READER 2: He taught students by the dozen.
Hard work was his second cousin.

READER 3: He had a prince to pay his bills,
One who loved his chords and trills.

ALL: The Father of the Symphony;
He lives on in our memory.

3. ONE OF TWELVE WHEN HE WAS BORN
("Surprise Symphony")

FRANZ JOSEPH HAYDN

Moderately fast, with marked rhythm (♩ = ca. 72)

mf crisply

mf

1. One of twelve when he was born; you would think he'd be for - lorn.
2. Folks who knew him in his day called him "Pa - pa," so they say.

Franz just took it in his stride; would not be de - nied.
Fa - ther of the sym - pho - ny; four move - ments, not three.

ff

Wolfgang Amadeus Mozart (1756-1791)

WOLFGANG AMADEUS MOZART was born on January 27, 1756, in Salzburg, Austria. His father was the official musician to the Archbishop of Salzburg; his mother was the prettiest woman in town. His parents lived in a modest third-floor apartment, but they gave their new baby son an impressive name: Johannes Chrysostomus Wolfgangus Theophilus Mozart. He preferred to be called Wolfgang Amadeus and even that seems like a mouthful.

From the very start, it was obvious that this was no ordinary child. The new Mozart baby boy was destined to be a child prodigy. Hearing a melody once, he could reproduce it without a single mistake. At the age of five he wrote a piano concerto that was too difficult for anyone to play. At seven he completed a sonata, at eight a symphony, and at age nine he wrote his first piece of music for a choir. He could easily improvise on a theme for half an hour without repeating himself. He sight read pieces perfectly.

His father, Leopold, recognized at once the possibility of fame and fortune for the Mozart family. He packed up the six-year old MOZART and his gifted sister, Nannerl, and took them on an extensive three-year European tour in which they performed before Kings and Queens. MOZART was considered by some to the Ninth Wonder of the World.

MOZART had many early successes, but found some decline in public interest as he grew out of childhood. In 1782, at the age of twenty-six, he went against his father's wishes and married Constanze Weber, his landlady's daughter. Although they were a happy couple, they had constant financial problems. MOZART was good at getting opportunities to play and at getting public recognition, but he was not good at getting paid for his work. He was a terrible businessman and, worse yet, he liked to gamble. Suddenly, he found himself a uniquely gifted musician with a wife and six children to feed and a run of bad luck. One of the most powerful musicians in Vienna, Antonio Salieri, did his best to put obstacles in the way of MOZART'S success, yet the Emperor and many members of the nobility continued to support MOZART'S operas.

MOZART died while he was still a young man, only thirty-five years old. He had only a few dollars to his name. A friend paid for his funeral on a bitter cold day, so cold that no one was at the graveside to say farewell. MOZART, the greatest musical genius to ever live, was buried in an unmarked grave.

During his brief and prolific career, he composed nearly fifty symphonies, nearly twenty operas, over twenty piano concertos, twenty-seven string quartets, almost forty violin sonatas plus much more chamber music. Some of his most famous works are *Eine Kleine Nachtmusik* (*A Little Night Music*), the operas *Don Giovanni* and *The Magic Flute* and his *40th Symphony*.

NARRATION

READER 1:	Mozart was a prodigy. Smart as any kid could be.
READER 2:	He played for Kings and Queens and such. Did they pay him? Well, not much!
READER 3:	A "Wonder of the World," some said. It may have gone to Mozart's head.
READER 4:	His music was so bright and sunny. Who could have known he needed money?
READER 5:	People hummed his minuets, But no one helped him pay his debts.
ALL:	He died so poor, it breaks our hearts . . . THE KING OF ALL THE CLASSIC CHARTS!

4. KING OF ALL THE CLASSIC CHARTS
(*from "Eine Kleine Nachtmusik"*)

WOLFGANG AMADEUS MOZART

1. From the start, the ver - y, ver - y start, it was clear this child was set a - part.
2. Thir - ty-five was all the years he got — pov - er - ty and bad luck were his lot.

At the ten - der age of five, they say, Mo - zart wrote a piece no - one could play!
Still his mu - sic lives with - in our hearts, He's the "King of all the clas - sic charts!"

No school for him, he toured the land. Great kings would shake his hand. He was a

Ludwig van Beethoven (1770~1827)

LUDWIG VAN BEETHOVEN was born on December 16, 1770, in Bonn, Germany. His father, Johann, was a singer and an alcoholic who wanted his young son to be a child prodigy like the great Mozart. Johann was his son's first music teacher, but he was often cruel and he forced BEETHOVEN to practice long hours to master his lessons.

At the age of four, BEETHOVEN could already play the clavier. By the age of eleven he quit school and, at thirteen, played the harpsichord at a local theatre. He was already conducting and composing music. At fourteen he became a student of the court organist, Christian Gottlob Neefe, and began to develop as a musician, becoming Neefe's paid assistant.

When BEETHOVEN was only seventeen, Mozart heard him play and said, "You will someday make a big noise in the world." Mozart was right — BEETHOVEN was destined to be a giant among composers.

In 1792, at the age of twenty-two, BEETHOVEN moved to Vienna where he studied with Haydn and Salieri, two of the greatest composers of that era. Unfortunately, BEETHOVEN was difficult to work with. He was stubborn and egotistical, which kept him from learning much from either teacher. He did become popular in Vienna as a concert pianist, but he had a bad temper and could be insulting at times. He once dumped a hot plate of veal and gravy over a poor waiter's head who brought him the wrong order. His servants constantly had to be replaced, and he was very sloppy in his dress and habits.

BEETHOVEN never married, but he always seemed to be in love with someone. He was not an easy man to love. Once he proposed to a court singer who refused him, saying he was "ugly and half-cracked."

The greatest tragedy of his life was his deafness. BEETHOVEN began to lose his hearing in his late twenties. Before he was fifty, he was totally deaf. This made it terribly difficult to compose music or communicate with people — and didn't help his temper. He wrote many works in his later years that he never heard at all. In 1824, in Vienna, BEETHOVEN conducted the premiere of his last symphony, the *Ninth*. The final movement ended, but the deaf BEETHOVEN (who was several measures off) continued to conduct, even as the audience applauded.

In spite of his terrible tantrums and lack of manners, he was one of the world's greatest musical geniuses and the very first composer to earn his living writing music. He wrote nine symphonies, thirty-two piano sonatas (including the *Moonlight Sonata*), seventeen string quartets, a Mass in D, one opera, *Fidelio*, and a wealth of chamber music.

In 1826, while visiting his brother, BEETHOVEN caught cold. Pneumonia followed along with further complications. He died in Vienna on March 26, 1827. The city mourned, schools were closed and thousands lined the streets to watch the funeral procession.

NARRATION

READER 1:   Ludwig! Ludwig! What a guy!
         He made a lot of people sigh.

READER 2:   No one ever called him lazy,
         But many people called him "CRAZY!"

READER 3:   His music broke the rules, it's true,
         But talents like his always do.

READER 4:   He couldn't hear. That made him mad.
         It made his temper more than bad.

READER 5:   But, ah, his music was so fine . . .
         Some people called it "just divine!"

ALL: Yes, he's a man we won't forget.
         Just listen to this "Minuet."

5. WHAT'S IT LIKE TO BE A PRODIGY?

("Minuet in G")

LUDWIG VAN BEETHOVEN

Lightly, with leisurely movement (♩ = 92-96)

1. What's it like to be a prod-i-gy? What's it like to be smart? What's it like to be a prod-i-gy, writ-ing mu-sic from the ver-y start? Well, if you want to know, ask some-one who's been there. What's it like to be a prod-i-gy? What's it

like to write a love-ly tune when you can't hear a note? What's it like to write a love-ly tune when your ears can't tell you what you wrote? Well, if you want to know, ask some-one who's been there. What's it like to write a love-ly tune when you

like to be smart? For in-stance, ask Lud-wig Bee-tho-ven; he would tell you that it's
can't hear a note? For in-stance, ask Lud-wig Bee-tho-ven; he would tell you it's no

hard; there is a lot of pres-sure ev-'ry min-ute, pres-sure ev-'ry day. What's a boy to
fun; you have to hear the sounds you're writ-ing in your head and not your ears. What's a guy to

do? It can make you cra-zy as a tick, make you mad, break your heart. It's like
do? It can make you cra-zy as a tick, make you mad, get your goat. It's like

na-ture plays a dirt-y trick when you're smart from the start. 2. What's it
na-ture plays a dirt-y trick when you can't hear a note.

Frederic Chopin (1810-1849)

FREDERIC CHOPIN was a child prodigy. He was born on March 1, 1810, in Zelazowa, Poland, to educated parents. By parentage he was half Polish and half French — and he spent about half his life in Warsaw and half in Paris. CHOPIN showed such unusual musical talent as a child that he was asked to perform a concerto at a public concert when he was only nine years old. He entered the Warsaw Conservatory at age sixteen to study music and had his first musical composition published that same year.

He became a piano student of Joseph Elsner, the director of the Conservatory and CHOPIN'S last teacher. Elsner both respected and encouraged CHOPIN'S individuality and personal style of writing. When CHOPIN left Poland in 1830, Elsner gave him a silver urn containing some Polish soil, urging CHOPIN to remember the land of his birth. It is said that what Poland meant to CHOPIN, CHOPIN'S music meant to Poland.

CHOPIN was an amazing performer at the keyboard, and soon he was giving concerts all over Europe: Vienna, Munich, Warsaw, Stuttgart and Paris. At that time, Paris was considered to be the "Capitol of Art," where CHOPIN met many famous musicians and was himself recognized as a musical genius. CHOPIN was known not only as a performer, but as a composer, and was a popular musical guest in the salons of French society.

Also in Paris, he fell in love with a celebrated writer Aurore Dudevant, who wrote under the name of George Sand. They were a very strange pair. CHOPIN was a frail, sickly, and fussy man while George was a hefty, strong, and outspoken woman who smoked cigars. She greatly influenced his life for many years. When he was thirty, he followed George and her children to the Island of Majorca where he became terribly ill.

From that time on his health was always poor, although he continued to play concerts until he died in Paris on October 17, 1849. Mozart's *Requiem* was performed at his funeral, as CHOPIN had requested. And the soil of his native Poland (from his teacher Elsner) was buried with him.

CHOPIN has been called "The Poet of the Piano." He made the piano a solo instrument. He introduced "rubato" playing, which meant using a flexible tempo rather than a steady beat. Also, CHOPIN especially liked to use the damper pedal to sustain notes. He was a brilliant pianist and his many keyboard works often used the themes of his native and beloved homeland, Poland.

NARRATION

READER 1:	Back in 1810, they say, Frederic Chopin claimed the day.
READER 2:	All the Polish folks could tell At the keyboard, he was SWELL!
READER 3:	He'd play piano day and night; His rising star was new and bright.
READER 4:	Everywhere he went they'd say, "Have YOU heard Freddy Chopin play?"
READER 5:	He fell in love beneath the stars. He called her George. She smoked cigars.
ALL:	His life was brief, we're sad to say. Like this little tune in the Key of A.

6. HE WAS A POLISH BOY
("Prelude in A")

FREDERIC CHOPIN

He was a Po - lish boy and mu - sic was his
went to gay Par - ee and fell in love, you

joy; Though he was small and meek, his tal - ents were u -
see; He called her George, they said; we bet she called him

nique. When he was nine, they say, he start-ed on his way — the
Fred. He nev-er went back home, was not in-clined to roam; but

pia - no was his claim to for-tune and to fame. He
Po - lish tunes were dear to him, as you can hear.

Johannes Brahms (1833~1897)

JOHANNES BRAHMS was born in Hamburg, Germany in 1833. His father was a mediocre musician and his mother was a seamstress, seventeen years older than her husband. They were an odd couple who didn't get along very well. The family had very little money, and BRAHMS grew up playing the piano in local taverns and bars to help pay the bills.

BRAHMS first studied piano when he was ten with Eduard Marxsen, one of the best music teachers in Hamburg. In 1853 he met the Hungarian violinist Eduard Remenyi, who invited the young man to tour with him as his accompanist. By the time BRAHMS was twenty both he and his brother were writing songs. When BRAHMS began to write serious music, he explored nearly every possible compositional form, with the exception of opera.

Some of his best known works are *The Academic Festival Overture*, his four symphonies, a set of waltzes called the *Liebeslieder Waltzes* and of course his most famous song *Wiegenlied*, which we call *Brahms' Lullaby*.

He enjoyed a life-long friendship with Robert Schumann, a well-known composer, and his wife Clara, a talented musician. They did a great deal to encourage, support and inspire BRAHMS.

BRAHMS never married. It is said by some that he thought of his songs as his children, and he called his four symphonies his "favorite sons." As he grew older, he became more and more strange in his habits and lifestyle. He had been a handsome young man who made the young girls' hearts flutter, but he became quite fat and sloppy as he grew older. He once attended a party where he shocked the ladies by arriving without any stockings.

BRAHMS spent the last twenty-six years of his life in Vienna, where he lived in a bachelor apartment and ate most of his meals in his favorite pub, The Red Hedgehog. He was known as "the great philosopher of music." He was a quiet, careful composer who stuck to the classical styles of the past and was not too interested in exploring new sounds and new musical ideas.

BRAHMS is one of the most famous of all composers. When we talk about "The Three B's" in music, we are referring to Bach, Beethoven and JOHANNES BRAHMS.

NARRATION

READER 1:   Brahms was born in Germany
In eighteen hundred thirty-three.

READER 2:   His father was a music man
And that's the way that Brahms began.

READER 3:   He had a gift for lovely tunes;
He played them in the town saloons.

READER 4:   But he loved serious music best.
He thought it was the loftiest.

READER 5:   His symphonies were only four;
Most people wish he'd written more.

ALL: This lullaby is one we know.
We're glad Brahms wrote it long ago.

7. WHEN YOU'RE SLEEPLESS IN HAMBURG
("Wiegenlied")

JOHANNES BRAHMS

Slowly and quietly (♩ = ca. 66)

Here's a tune you can hum when you're toss - ing and
when you've count - ed your

turn - ing; here's a tune that you can hum when you just can't close your
last sheep; when the moon is on the

Peter Ilyich Tchaikovsky (1840-1893)

Of all the Russian composers, TCHAIKOVSKY is the best known. He was born on May 7, 1840, in Votkinsk, a small town in eastern Russia. He studied music when he was quite young with his mother and then a local piano teacher. At the age of ten he was sent to boarding school in St. Petersburg and became very homesick. Four years later his mother, whom he adored, died of cholera.

TCHAIKOVSKY'S father was a mining inspector who wanted something better for his son. He insisted that TCHAIKOVSKY study law and sent him to the School of Jurisprudence. At nineteen, Peter completed his studies and spent three years as a law clerk at the Ministry of Justice.

He loved living in the city with all the concerts, performances and parties, but he hated his work. He decided to enroll for free classes in Music Theory at the Musical Society in town. He realized then that he was meant to be a composer, not a lawyer.

It was a good thing that Anton Rubinstein, the Director of the Conservatory, visited TCHAIKOVSKY'S classes. He was impressed with Peter's talent and encouraged him to enroll at the Conservatory. Rubinstein became his teacher, friend, adviser and critic for many years to come.

TCHAIKOVSKY graduated from the Conservatory in 1865. Soon after, he won a silver medal for one of his cantatas. Before long, he was invited to teach at the Conservatory and began to fulfill his destiny as a composer. His first masterwork was completed in 1869 — the orchestral fantasy-overture *Romeo and Juliet*.

Composers and artists often live in terrible poverty. TCHAIKOVSKY was no different. Just when things were getting desperate, a wealthy widow, Madame von Meck, offered to support him. Although they never met in person, she paid his bills and was his best friend for many years. He married Antonina Miliukova in 1877, but they separated after eleven weeks.

TCHAIKOVSKY had many emotional problems. He feared that his head might slip off his shoulders when he conducted an orchestra, so he would hold up his chin with his left hand while conducting.

His moodiness is reflected in his music, which includes the ballets *Swan Lake* and *The Nutcracker*, six symphonies and symphonic works like *The 1812 Overture* and *The Slavonic March*. He died of cholera (tainted water) in St. Petersburg, a few days after he had conducted his *Sixth Symphony*. He was only fifty-three years old.

NARRATION

READER 1:
Tchaikovsky was a Russian lad,
An awkward boy and often sad.

READER 2:
His father sent him off to school.
His mother died and life seemed cruel.

READER 3:
He tried to study law, they said,
But tunes kept running through his head.

READER 4:
So, he chose music. He'd compose.
Perhaps some oratorios?

READER 5:
He found his style. He found his niche.
Though music never made him rich.

ALL:
He's famous now. So just remember:
You'll always hear him in December.

8. HOW WOULD YOU LIKE TO HAVE A MIDDLE NAME LIKE ILYICH?

(*Themes from* "The Nutcracker")

PETER ILYICH TCHAIKOVSKY

Lightly with movement (♩ = ca. 80)

mf marcato

How would you like to have a mid-dle name like Il-yich? *

How would you like to have to spell *that* each and ev-'ry day?

And what if you were born in Rus-sia, could you take it?

*Note: There seem to be a variety of spellings of Tchaikovsky's middle name. Some variations are "Ilich" and "Iljitch."

(*Pronounced: ill-ee-itch*)

Call it "The Nut-crack-er," and some-one fa-mous could be you!

9. CLOSING FANFARE

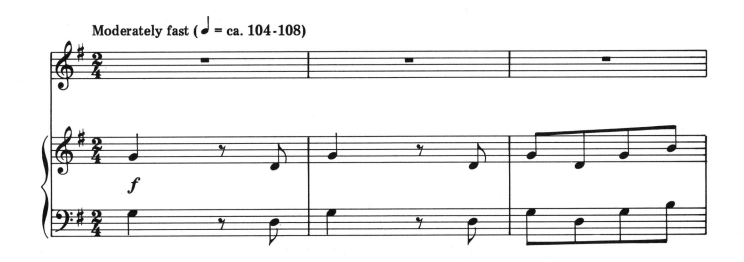

Moderately fast (♩ = ca. 104-108)

Now we're fin-ished, now we're done.

Glad you came to share the fun.

We hope _____ you will re-mem-ber _____ the sev-en

guys who gave us tunes we can't for - get.

WHAT'S MY NUMBER?

Let's call our favorite composers on the composer hotline. What numbers will you dial to reach each of them? Be careful, because each number represents several letters of the alphabet.

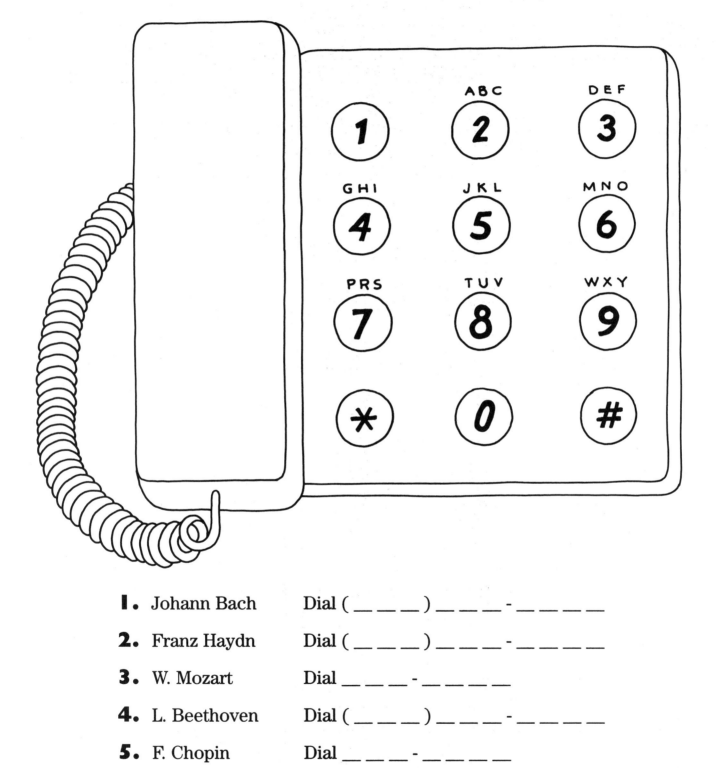

1. Johann Bach Dial (__ __ __) __ __ __ - __ __ __ __

2. Franz Haydn Dial (__ __ __) __ __ __ - __ __ __ __

3. W. Mozart Dial __ __ __ - __ __ __ __

4. L. Beethoven Dial (__ __ __) __ __ __ - __ __ __ __

5. F. Chopin Dial __ __ __ - __ __ __ __

6. J. Brahms Dial __ __ __ - __ __ __ __

7. Tchaikovsky Dial __ (__ __ __) __ __ __ - __ __ __ __

GET ME TO THE CHURCH ON TIME

They say that Bach once walked 200 miles to hear Dietrich Buxtehude play a concert on the organ. Can you get Bach to the concert on time? (We suggest using a colored pencil to find your way.)

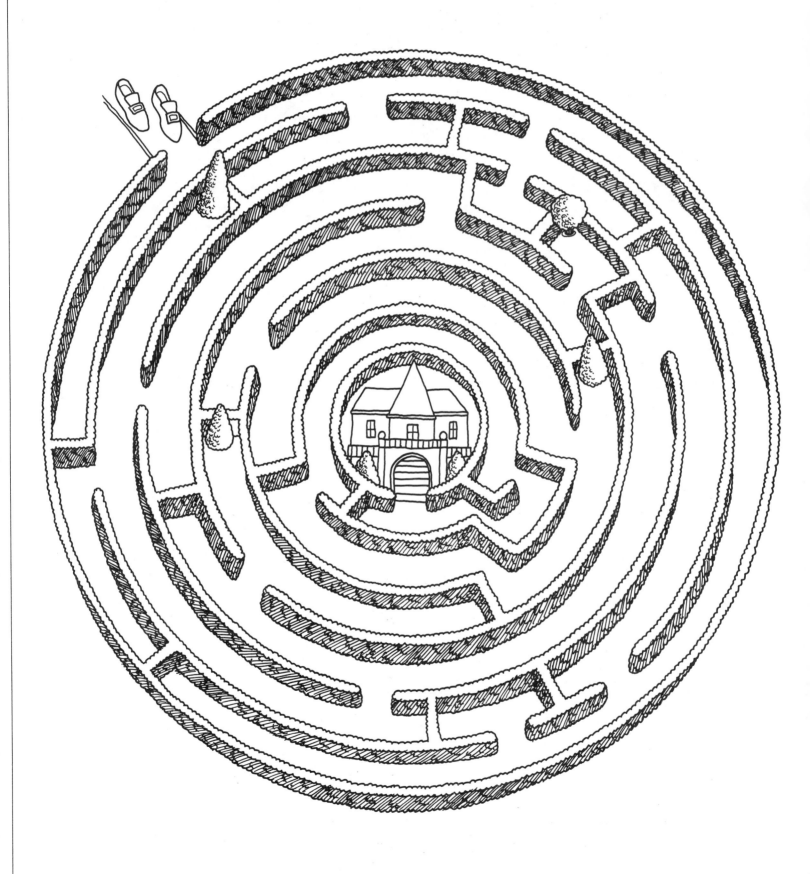

CAN WE TALK?

Here are some things to think about and to talk about in your class.

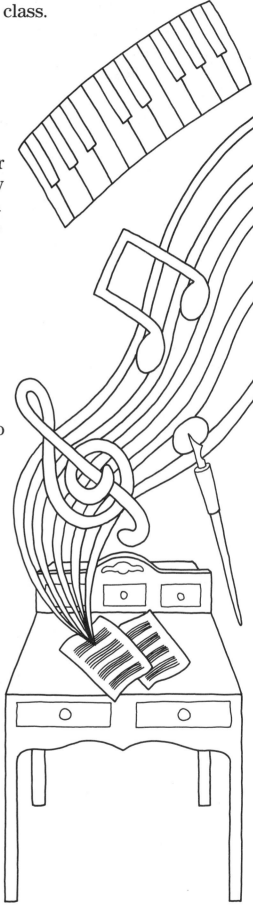

1. How does a composer think and work? Some composers, like Mozart, work everything out in their heads before they ever write a single note. It makes their writing seem so easy. Others, like Brahms, work very hard and rewrite everything many times. Brahms often got so upset with his music that he tore it up after working on it for months. It is for this reason that many of his compositions were never heard by anyone. When Beethoven was asked where he got his ideas he said he wasn't sure where they came from.

   What do you think? If you were a composer how would you begin writing a piece of music?

2. What exactly is a "prodigy?" You will notice that many famous composers were prodigies or child geniuses. Do you know anybody you think is a prodigy or a genius?

   What about famous people who became stars when they were very young? Can you think of any? Would you call them prodigies? Why or why not?

3. Each of us has handicaps. Some of them are easier to deal with than others. Beethoven had a handicap to deal with later in his life, when he began to lose his hearing. How could he write music if he couldn't hear what he was writing? They say that he once conducted a concert and continued conducting even after the orchestra was finished playing because he couldn't hear them at all.

   Can you think of any famous people today who have overcome physical handicaps to become great? How about Stevie Wonder, or Ray Charles, or Helen Keller? Can you name some others?

T-TIME

Do you have good ideas for artistic designs? Here's your chance. Design a T-shirt for your favorite composer. Write a catchy slogan to go with the shirt. For example, you could design a shirt with the word "Mozart" and a crown, adding the slogan "King of All the Classic Charts." Good luck!

WHERE IN THE WORLD ARE WE?

Can you find the birthplaces of these famous composers? Draw a line from the composer's name to the city where he was born.

J. S. Bach   Tchaikovsky

Haydn

Mozart

Brahms   Beethoven   Chopin

BOOKS! BOOKS! BOOKS!

Does your school or local library have many books about music and composers?
See how many books you can find on the following subjects:

Music History	Beethoven	Mozart
Bach	Chopin	Tchaikovsky
Brahms	Haydn	Others?

TITLE	AUTHOR	PUBLISHER	COPYRIGHT	NO. OF PAGES

ART WORKS

Draw a picture of your favorite composer featured in this collection as he might look at work, at home or on the streets of his favorite city. Sign your drawing in the lower right-hand corner.

SCRAMBLED EGGS, ANYONE?

Well, not quite. But maybe "scrambled composers!"
Can you unscramble the names of these composer giants?

1. HABC   _ _ _ _ _

2. PICOHN   _ _ _ _ _ _

3. RAMZOT   _ _ _ _ _ _

4. NYHAD   _ _ _ _ _

5. EHTENEBOV   _ _ _ _ _ _ _ _ _

6. MARBHS   _ _ _ _ _ _

7. KSTHCAVYIOK   _ _ _ _ _ _ _ _ _ _ _

FIND THESE WORDS

How many of these 30 words and names can you find in this maze of letters?
They appear forward, backward, across, up, down and diagonal.

BACH
BALLET
BEETHOVEN
BRAHMS
BRANDENBURG
CHOIR

CHOPIN
CLAVICHORD
COMPOSER
CONCERTO
GEORGE
HARPSICHORD

HAYDN
LULLABY
MAGIC FLUTE
MINUET
MOZART
MUSIC

NUTCRACKER
OPERA
ORGAN
OVERTURE
PIANO
PRELUDE

PRODIGY
QUARTET
SCALE
SYMPHONY
TCHAIKOVSKY
TUNE

```
L  G  R  U  B  N  E  D  N  A  R  B  S  C  Q  G  H  I
A  R  A  R  O  T  R  E  C  N  O  C  O  U  L  M  J  E
F  E  D  B  H  A  Y  D  N  F  A  K  A  L  P  Z  Q  R
B  S  C  M  Q  L  N  I  E  L  K  R  M  R  M  N  Y  U
H  O  B  A  C  H  P  M  E  M  T  H  O  N  E  D  L  T
A  P  G  G  M  O  I  G  L  E  N  D  Z  O  Y  Y  P  R
R  M  K  I  H  J  A  O  T  E  I  R  A  R  K  X  T  E
P  O  L  C  B  Q  N  P  V  G  Q  O  R  W  S  C  E  V
S  C  B  F  A  H  O  O  Y  L  R  H  T  V  V  P  U  O
I  H  J  L  L  U  H  O  H  Y  S  C  H  S  O  F  N  O
C  J  C  U  L  T  V  U  N  B  T  I  S  E  K  D  I  J
H  Z  Y  T  E  W  X  O  P  A  Q  V  M  M  I  K  M  I
O  I  H  E  T  V  H  R  G  L  N  A  H  H  A  I  O  L
R  Z  B  E  X  P  G  G  F  L  A  L  A  G  H  B  P  N
D  E  N  Y  M  W  R  A  N  U  T  C  R  A  C  K  E  R
F  U  Z  Y  R  I  Y  N  E  L  W  X  B  P  T  Y  R  A
T  A  S  Y  O  Q  A  T  U  E  G  R  O  E  G  W  A  T
B  D  Z  H  S  C  F  V  M  U  S  I  C  Q  F  R  D  S
C  E  C  A  B  X  W  Y  V  T  P  R  E  L  U  D  E  A
```

WORD SEARCH

Beethoven wasn't able to hear in the later years of his life, but there was nothing wrong with his eyesight. How is yours? How many words can you make out of the letters in BEETHOVEN's name? Each word should use a minimum of three letters.

LUDWIG VAN BEETHOVEN

WHO'S IN THE NEWS?

Write a brief history of your favorite composer. If you have a school newspaper, you may be able to submit this biography to be included in one of the issues. Be sure your history includes these basic facts:

1. Date and place of birth and death

2. Nationality

3. Period in music history

4. Types of music written

5. At least five interesting facts about his life

6. One or two well-known compositions

7. The name of a library book about his life—mention the title, the author, the copyright date and the number of pages

8. Add an eye-catching headline to your article

♪ *The* **DAILY NOTE** ♫

25¢   CURRENT ISSUE   25¢

WHO AM I?

If you heard these composers talking about themselves, could you guess who is speaking from what they say?

1. I cannot hear the music I write. Who am I? _____

2. I have 20 children. Who am I? _____

3. My friends call me "Papa." Who am I? _____

4. I wrote the Nutcracker Suite. Who am I? _____

5. When I was five, I wrote a piece of music that was so difficult, no one could play it. Who am I? _____

6. I was called "The Father of the Symphony." Who am I? _____

7. I call my girlfriend George. Who am I? _____

8. Some people think I'm the "Ninth Wonder of the World." Who am I?
_____

9. I wrote the best-known lullaby in the world. Who am I?
_____

10. I often write a tune a week to play in my church. Who am I?
_____

11. Your keyboard is tuned the way it is today because of me. Who am I?
_____

12. I taught Mozart and Beethoven. Who am I? _____

13. I was first schooled as a lawyer. Who am I? _____

14. I conducted the premiere of my last symphony. Who am I?
_____

15. I was a popular musician in the salons of Paris. Who am I?
_____

YOU'RE A GRAND OLD FLAG

Our seven featured composers represent four different countries. Some of them come from the same country. Can you fill in the country's name after each composer?

COMPOSERS   COUNTRIES

BACH   _____

BEETHOVEN   _____

BRAHMS   _____

CHOPIN   _____

HAYDN   _____

MOZART   _____

TCHAIKOVSKY   _____

Color in these nations' flags with the right colors. You may need to check an encyclopedia to find the colors for each national flag. Good luck!

AUSTRIA   GERMANY

POLAND   RUSSIA

NUTCRACKER ART

Listen to the music of the *Nutcracker Suite*. Read the story. If you have an opportunity during the holiday season, go to see a production of the *Nutcracker*. Now, draw a picture of your favorite scene. Label the scene.